Get A Job In

30 Days

Destiny S. Harris

...

Copyright

Copyright © 2023 Destiny S. Harris.

Front cover image by Destiny S. Harris.
Book design by Destiny S. Harris.
First printing edition 2023.
www.destinyh.com

...

. . .

Dedication

For everyone looking for the next best job that can change their life, financial outcomes, and overall life satisfaction.

...

. . .

A Gift For You

Thank you for taking the time to read this book. As a token of my appreciation, here is a gift to you.

I give away free books daily. Here's how to get your free books today:

Step 1: Visit

amazon.com/author/destinyharris

Step 2: Filter books by "Price: Low to High"

Step 3: Download available free ebooks

. . .

. . .

Table of Contents

. . .

...

Quick Bit

Thank you for taking the time to read this book.

My hope is that you leave at least 1% better than before you read this book and walk away with at least one takeaway.

I'd like to graciously ask that you help me by leaving a <u>review</u> of this book; your feedback helps me write better books and helps others get a glimpse of the book.

With Kindness,
Destiny

...

. . .

Get A Job In 30 Days Or Less

Getting a job in thirty days or less might seem daunting, but it's more than possible.

How do I know?

I've done it multiple times.

This book is going to teach you everything you need to do to get a job, but if you want to get it in 30 days or less, there are a few things you need to do on top of what follows in this book:

Before the 30-day journey begins

- Ensure your resume is solid before you start the 30-day application process.

The resume (and LinkedIn) are critical elements and the first peek into your candidacy.

Ensure both of these are on point.

- Are there any certifications you can attain quickly?

If so, acquire them and put the credentials behind your name on email signatures, your resume, your applications, and your LinkedIn profile.

- Before you start the 30-day job process, apply to 1,000 jobs.

You can get this done in 1 week or less; this step is essential because it positions you to have interviews lined up before you begin the thirty-day journey.

- Become skillful at interviewing.

There is little room for blowing interviews if you want to lock down an offer by the 30-day mark.

You **can** use some companies (since you're applying to thousands) as practice, but you want to consistently conduct interviews at this point, which means doing what is necessary to prepare yourself before the 30-day journey commences.

After the 30-day journey commences

- Apply to 100-300 jobs daily.

- Network like a MF; cold message about 10-100 people daily to put out leads and increase your chances for a referral or way into a company.

- Reach out to the hiring manager/team when you submit your resume for the job and introduce yourself.

This makes you stand out slightly more from the rest of the applicants.

- Submit a thank you note with every job application you submit.

- Submit a thank you note after every interview.

- Do not get phased/emotional by rejections; stay focused and continue applying.

- Reach out to potential employers that contact you within 24 hours or less.

- Ensure your resume is tailored and has the job keywords throughout the resume.

During the thirty-day job hunt, you should have interviews lined up weekly, daily, or almost daily.

If you find the thirty-day timeline too aggressive, extend it by one month to give yourself more time.

The rest of the content in this book will prepare your candidate profile and give you the know-how to succeed in your thirty-day or general job search.

Good luck!

...

. . .

Introduction

I have worked with thousands of students throughout my teaching career, which commenced in 2007, and people frequently ask me for career advice.

Since so many people constantly asked for advice and I recognized the knowledge gap with people trying to get a job or transition to a better one, I finally decided to write a book to compile all my career hacks.

Here, you will find the most valuable pieces of advice I have been sharing with my students, friends, and family to help them experience a successful career and get the desired job.

I wish you much success in nailing your dream job, career, or next transitional step.

Cheers.

...

. . .

Chapter 1: Your Resume

The Resume

Aside from your LinkedIn, your resume is the first step to your candidacy.

Think of the resume (and your LinkedIn profile) as part of the "first date experience.

You know how you try to find all the information you can about someone before that first date (which is essentially the interview)?

Your resume (and LinkedIn profile) is your social media profile for your job hunt.

It is **imperative** you succeed in creating a solid resume for yourself.

Excellent resumes attract longer reviews from recruiters and hiring managers, exciting conversations, *more* career opportunities, *quality* career opportunities, and higher pay.

Standout With Design

Most people have a regular and boring resume.

It's the same resume that everyone else has.

If I were a recruiter, I would pay more attention to a resume with a slightly different appeal versus a resume with the same layout as many are.

The design won't matter for some jobs, but why not put a little more effort into making an aesthetically pleasing resume?

It doesn't have to have every color of the rainbow or be a masterpiece.

But having a layout that pops out to the naked eye and makes a statement can't hurt you

There are thousands of resume templates and layouts available for free.

Find one that resonates with your personality and make your mark with it.

Grammar

Please get this right.

I run my resume through spell check and Grammarly, *and* read it aloud several times, and I've still missed stuff!

Don't mess up the grammar.

People who care will notice mistakes.

People who don't care will notice mistakes.

And potential employers try to knock people off the list for anything they can.

You will run into employers that give you a break; these usually end up being the best employers, too.

<u>Organization</u>

Layout *matters.*

Make sure the layout of your resume makes sense and displays your experience in an organized fashion.

<u>Here are some simple tips that make all the
difference:</u>

- Keep the number of bullet points the same
for each position.

- Place the title, company, date, and location on
one line.

- Use "Professional Experience," *not* "Work
Experience," "Experience," or "Job History," as
a section divider before you delve into all of
your experience.

You also don't have to use a title for this
section.

- Place your "Professional Summary" at the top
of your resume.

Keep this crisp, short, sweet, and enticing.

- Add your LinkedIn profile URL to the top of your resume under your contact info.

- Do not put your full address on your resume.

- Do not put your GPA on your resume.

- Don't include your picture on your resume unless it has proven to be successful for *you*. You want to avoid as much unconscious and unintentional bias as possible.

Dates

Don't include the months you've worked at past positions.

Only include years.

You can get to dates if the employer asks during an interview or on a background check, but there is no need to lay all your cards out on the table initially.

Hobbies & Passion Projects

Share something unique about yourself.

Include some passion projects or hobbies you engage in regularly.

Show your human elements.

It's not only about what you can do for an employer but also about who you are.

Display some personality in your resume.

File Name

Avoid using "JohnDoeResume" instead, use something *different* that stands out (e.g., "AmbitiousCandidate_JohnDoe."

Final Thoughts

You want your resume to stand out, be crisp, be modern, and look like you've put a substantial effort into it.

The worst thing to have as a professional is an ugly resume.

Put some effort into your resume!

I always encourage my students to look at several resume examples from professionals in their desired field.

You can google resumes or look up top professionals on LinkedIn to see how they build their resumes.

Learn from the experts.

You don't need to reinvent the wheel here because it's already been created.

Now, you just need to refine your wheel and make it worthy of a second take.

. . .

. . .

Chapter 2: Your LinkedIn

Your resume and LinkedIn profile are the first pit stops for potential employers and recruiters.

Match It Up

They don't have to match up perfectly, but your resume and LinkedIn profile should have an unmistakable resemblance.

Some people put more information on their LinkedIn profiles; others put more information on their resumes.

Do what works best for you and your goals.

But keep the resume and LinkedIn profile in sync with one another.

About

Make the About section interesting, eccentric, and *you.*

It can be long, or it can be short.

If you have a long "about" summary, be sure to have a short summary at the top for people who don't have the time (or don't desire to take the time) to read a long summary.

Picture

Have a **GOOD** picture.

It may not need to be professional (depending on the type of job or company you are going for), but it should be clear and presentable.

Keep it interesting!

Background

Choose something that matters to you for your LinkedIn background.

You can also change it regularly to keep your page fresh, engaging, and buzzing with change.

Fill Her Up

Make use of all the sections on your profile page that you can.

List your education, certifications, courses, volunteer organizations, awards, projects, and work you have completed that you're proud to showcase.

Years

Be sure only to put down the **years** of your employment.

You don't need to put months and days.

Remember, you can give more details as you progress in the interview process.

Get to know each other better first before spilling all the beans.

Plus, it displays a cleaner look when you only show the years.

Certifications

If you have relevant certifications, put them behind your last name (e.g., Lina Thompson, CPM, PMP); this adds more credibility and visibility to your credentials.

Recommendations

Give out recommendations to your peers. Share and spread the love.

Share The *Right* Information

Some information you simply don't need to share. I will leave this up to your discretion to determine.

. . .

. . .

Chapter 3: Your Email Address

Tip: Make your email address POP.

The little things count.

Instead of "johndoe@gmail.com," try "choosejohndoe@gmail.com" or "selectjohndoc@gmail.com."

Get creative and make your email address stand out.

People will always ask about it and take a second look at it.

Anything that helps you stand out can increase your chances of nailing your desired job.

The little details add up!

. . .

...

Chapter 4: Your Leads

One of the first questions I always ask anyone who says they're looking for a job is:

How many jobs are you applying to per day?

<u>Usually, people will give one of the following replies:</u>

1. A couple per week
2. 1-3 jobs per day
3. I haven't been really applying

These answers don't cut it.

I *always* recommend applying for anywhere from 10 to 100 jobs per day.

In this way, you can plant 100 seeds (new leads) every couple of days, daily, or weekly.

To make the most out of your job search, apply to numerous jobs consistently.

It should not be a part-time thing unless you are *not* earnestly looking to get a job anytime soon (or you might have a very high in-demand profile, which means you can get away with doing less work).

Tip: Commit to applying to at least 100 jobs every few days or every 5-7 days.

The more seeds you plant, the higher your return will be.

Tip 2: The higher the quality of your applications you submit, the more you increase your chances of getting an interview or moving to the next step.

Plant Your Seeds In The Morning

Put out your applications in the morning before the workday starts.

This way your applications and emails can be at the top of a potential employer's list or inbox.

Keep Track

I think most of us have all had that moment where we get a call back from an employer we forgot we applied to, and for some reason, we struggle to find it in our inbox.

One way to avoid this is to keep track of all the jobs you apply to in a spreadsheet.

It doesn't take much time; it's worth it and keeps you organized.

<u>Things To Track:</u>

1. Company

2. Title

3. Interviews (Dates, Times, Interviewers)

4. People you network with on LinkedIn or email

. . .

. . .

Chapter 5: Your Thank You

A thank you here and a thank you there will always take you further than a thank you nowhere.

Follow up on conversations and interviews with customized, professional, and memorable thank-you notes.

In your thank you notes, aim to mention at least one thing from the conversation that interested both of you (it doesn't need to be work-related; it just needs to be memorable and thoughtful).

One of my students submits personalized thank you videos with each one of his applications.

You don't need to do this, but the thought always counts.

Those who go above and beyond with their thoughtfulness usually get rewarded compared to the average person.

When you have a networking conversation with someone, send them a thank you note.

When you complete an interview, send a thank you note.

When you get your interview set up, send a thank you note to the coordinator.

When you get feedback from a potential employer, send a thank you note.

Anytime you can, send a thank you note.

Kindness will *always* take you further in your career—in *every* aspect.

All the people you have conversations with are taking time out of their days to speak with you—whether it is their job or not.

So, take the time to appreciate them, and they will usually take the time to appreciate you.

There is something magical about the power of gratitude.

See what it does for your life after zealously implementing it into your career search.

. . .

. . .

Chapter 6: Your Interview

Make sure you are applying to jobs from day 1.

Do not avoid applying to jobs because you feel you are not ready, do not have enough experience, or feel any other excuse you might have.

If your interview skills are lacking, practice, practice, practice.

Practice

Think of every interview you complete as a practice round.

You have nothing to lose but everything to gain.

Practice always makes you better.

Record Yourself

Record your interviews.

When you record your interviews, you can analyze your responses and gestures and learn how the interviewer responds to you.

When you have a record of your responses, you can hone your knowledge and answers to make them better for the following interview.

Create A Script

If you are applying for a job in a specific field, many of the questions you receive will be similar; this is great for you!

Because now, you can create a document or spreadsheet of your answers to these questions and practice communicating them orally and verbally!

Over time, you will easily remember your answers and freestyle them in interviews or written pre-screenings.

Many written interview questions you will receive will be similar, so having a dedicated location for the questions you receive and your answers will save you time.

Read The Interviewer

Some interviewers like to stay in control of the interview and have a list of questions (essentially a script) they would like to stick to.

Other interviews are more flexible and let the conversation develop organically.

Others won't mind if you take control of the interview (though they may not say it overtly).

Don't take control when the interviewer clearly wouldn't like that, and don't be boring when the interviewer is fun.

Match your energy to the interviewer.

Interview The Interviewer

This is your life, too, you know.

You need to interview the company and person interviewing you to make sure *they* are a good fit for *you.*

It's not *only* about you being a good fit for them.

<u>Here are some solid questions to ask:</u>

1. How would you describe the culture of this company?

2. How would you describe the people who work here?

3. What hours do people usually work?

4. Do people move around in the company?

5. What is the employee churn rate?

6. How long have people usually worked at this company?

7. What is your favorite thing about working here?

8. What is your least favorite thing about working here?

9. Do people have a lot of flexibility in this company?

10. Are you all a meeting-driven company or an action-oriented company?

Ask Questions That Focus On Adding Value

Be sure to make yourself look good in the interview by asking how you can add value to the company.

Focus on being an asset, and people will be more excited about you joining their company.

Here are some example questions to ask:

1. How can I add value to the company within the first six months?

2. What are the most important things I can do within the first 90 days of starting this role?

3. What are some pain points the team is facing or experiencing?

4. How would you rate the team collaboration levels?

<u>Learn Your Manager QUICKLY!</u>

A manager can break or make your position.

Some managers are micromanagers, some are macro-managers, some focus on mentorship and professional development, and some managers will be your friends.

Know what type of manager you want.

<u>Here are some questions to ask a potential manager:</u>

1. How would you describe your management style?

2. What are your pet peeves for direct reports?

3. What expectations do you set with all of your direct reports?

4. What about my background sticks out to you?

5. What do you like to do outside of work?

Note: this is a critical one; if they don't have a life outside of work, they might end up making *you* their life = micromanaging

6. What brought you to this company?

7. How long do you intend to stay at this company?

Getting a superb manager is awesome unless they leave shortly after you join.

8. How can I add value to the team within my first six months of arrival?

. . .

. . .

Chapter 7: Your Salary

You established the amount of money you desire to be paid at the beginning of this book.

Now that you know what you desire to be paid, it's consequential to ask yourself, is your rate the going market price for your desired role?

It's time to do some research.

Research Your Salary & Field

Take some time to explore the going salary for people in your field.

Is your target over, under, or right on the money?

It does not matter if you are over the market salary if you believe you deserve this rate.

But it **does** matter if you are *under* the market rate.

Never work for someone else getting paid less than you deserve.

This will waste time and money for you and your future.

You lose out on so much money by taking a salary lower than what you could be making (each year, you lose thousands of dollars when you are underpaid, and it's a cumulative effect on the rest of your career).

Stay in tune with the market rate to ensure you get paid *above* average.

Keep It To Yourself

If you can, don't give your salary at the beginning of the interview process; keep this information to yourself to make a more informed decision.

Many potential employers will try to get you to give the first number but don't budge; wait and feel out the opportunity first.

Always Give A Range

When the time comes for you to give your number, give a 10-15k range.

Make the lowest end of the range the minimum you will accept; in this way, you can't be disappointed if the employer decides to meet your most minimal salary demands.

Don't Play The Fool

Example 1: Let's say you were looking at working at a startup.

They say they will pay you 80k as a senior product manager (despite the going rate being six figures). Their excuse is that they are a startup and must keep their overhead low.

Instead, they will give you equity or a stake in the company.

Some people will be entirely on board with this; however, it is critical to find out as much as you can about the workload and reliability of the company since it's a startup.

Usually, the workload at a startup is more intense than an established enterprise.

If a startup ardently wants you, they will find a way to pay for you.

So be sure not to settle just because a company tells you your rate is out of range; there is usually always wiggle room for the most attractive candidates.

Example 2: If you give your rate and they end up coming back offering you more than you asked for, this most likely means that you asked for less than you could have received.

Let this be a lesson.

You are reading this book, so you can't be tricked now!

<u>Salary Tools</u>

Some great sites and tools you can use to determine what your rate should be are listed below.

There are tons of resources available; I am only giving a few of the popular ones:

1. LinkedIn
2. Glassdoor
3. Salary.com
4. PayScale

...

. . .

Chapter 8: Your Education

<u>Education</u>

First off, you don't need a degree to get a job.

If anyone tells you differently, they have an outdated mentality.

If you don't like school or don't want to go back to school, then *don't*.

But know, you *may* need to get creative and compensate for the lack of it in other areas (e.g., professional experience).

However, many employers don't give a sh*t about education anymore.

Many employers want to know you can execute on the job and add value to their company.

I have three degrees, but I realize that one, two, or three degrees don't make me more intelligent or better than anyone.

It's what we *do* with the knowledge we have that leads us to better opportunities than others.

Certifications

These will be your best friends.

Get as many as possible to benefit you and your career goals.

Try to get the low-cost ones on your own and the higher-priced certifications paid for by your employer. Or get both paid for by your employer -- even better!

Many of the certifications I completed occurred early in my career when I wasn't allocating my time to other areas of life.

If you don't have much time to allocate and don't have any certifications, there are some quick and easy ways to get them.

One of my students studied for an exam and took the exam within a couple of days.

Now, she is certified in her field.

LinkedIn Learning

This platform provides thousands of courses and certifications you can take to become an expert in your field.

Some courses are only a few minutes long; others last for hours.

The cool thing about LinkedIn Learning is that it only costs you $30/month, and you can take and complete as many courses as you want.

Whenever you complete a course, you also receive a certification to add to your LinkedIn profile and resume.

At one point, I had a page of my resume dedicated to the hundreds of courses I took.

This sparked some valuable conversations about my passion for growing and adding value to whichever company I am employed.

Always Be Learning

This applies not only to your career but also to your life.

The better you are as a person, the better you will be as an employee.

Focus on holistic self-development, which includes both professional and personal development.

. . .

. . .

Chapter 9: Your Network

The easiest way to get a job is by networking and referrals.

If you ever notice, when a new leadership person comes into a company, they usually bring in all these new people **they *know.***

Let this be a clear sign for you to network and make new connections as a way of life.

Check-in on people, send them holiday greetings, ask them if you can help in their career, and be a genuine resource and friend to people.

If people know they can count on you for sincere conversation and have been in contact with you frequently, they will have no problem helping you in the future if *you* ever need it.

The people who get the jobs the easiest are the people who make valuable connections.

These people don't need a resume, the certifications, the education, and sometimes not even an interview.

Make the connections and check in on your connections regularly.

Don't be the person that only contacts someone when they need something.

. . .

. . .

Chapter 10: Your Style

One of my students creates a personalized video he sends to every company he applies to.

He also sends a personalized introduction video to a team lead in the department he desires to work in.

Finally, he submits a project deliverable to the company that solves an issue the company faces.

He does all of this before even landing a formal interview.

And guess what?

He never encounters trouble landing a new job.

Each person will have their own strategies for standing out, but make sure you *have* a strategy to stand out.

Be someone that doesn't just submit an application and wait to hear back.

Proactive Applications

Be proactive in the application process.

Reach out to someone at the company and let them know you applied.

Add your portfolio link to your application so potential employers can see your work.

Send a thank you note with every application, conveying your gratitude for their time and efforts in reviewing your application.

Reach out to other people at the company you desire to work for and have chats about their experiences working there.

Go above the bar, and the sky will *always* be your limit.

So many people today are getting incredibly creative with their applications and finding lucrative success.

It takes more time to go above and beyond, but it is worth it.

Just implementing some of the things I mentioned above is good enough to do.

The goal is to take action and create the best opportunities you can for yourself in your job search by going above the bar.

. . .

...

Thank You For Reading

Thank you for reading this book.

Stay loved, blessed, lucky, favored, aware, joyous, and committed to bettering yourself.

. . .

...

The End.

...

. . .

About Destiny S. Harris

Destiny S. Harris' goal is to positively inspire, cultivate, elevate, and educate the minds of individuals across the globe through her writing.

Creating (whether books, courses, articles, poetry, or music) has always been Destiny's thing, not to mention health & fitness and all things entrepreneurial.

Destiny published her first book, "Beauty Secrets for Girls," at age 11 and her second book, "Don't Wait Until It's Too Late," at age 12.

Destiny obtained three degrees in Psychology, Political Science, & Women's Studies. She also started her own music teaching business at the age of 14, which she led for over ten years. In addition, she has been teaching academic, career, and personal development topics to thousands of students and readers since 2004.

Outside of writing, Destiny loves and enjoys a few other things: reading, weightlifting, walking, biking, traveling, football, dogs, animals, food, classic movies, mountain and ocean views, sleeping, plants, and nature.

Check out her work, leave a review, share your thoughts with your friends and family, and be a part of a movement: helping people learn and grow through means of self-education (books).

<u>Complete the Steps To Get Free eBooks:</u>

Step 1: Go to

amazon.com/author/destinyharris

Step 2: Filter books by "Price: Low to High"

Step 3: Download available free books

...

Connect W/ Destiny S. Harris

Please reach out and stay in touch. Start a conversation today @ destinyh.com

...

...

Free Gifts!

Access courses & free eBooks at the link below:

destinyh.com

. . .

Please Leave A Review

If this book impacts you in some way, please let me know by dropping a review on it.

I write better books with **your** input.

. . .

Tell Me What You Want

I've written many books, but if you don't see what you're looking for or need, get in touch with me via my website, articles, comments, or reviews, and let me know what you're looking for so I can create it for you. I'm here to serve.

Love,

Destiny

...

. . .

www.ingramcontent.com/pod-product-compliance
Lightning Source LLC
Chambersburg PA
CBHW031402250726
48656CB00002B/532